EATING
MY
WORDS

For Zadie, Elaina, and Teddy —B.P.C.

Some poems included in this volume were previously published in *Rainbow Soup: Adventures in Poetry* (© 2004), *Rhyme and PUNishment: Adventures in Wordplay* (© 2006), *The Laugh Stand: Adventures in Humor* (© 2008), *If It Rains Pancakes: Haiku and Lantern Poems* (© 2014), *Ode to a Commode: Concrete Poems* (© 2015), *Something Sure Smells Around Here: Limericks* (© 2015), *Bow-Tie Pasta: Acrostic Poems* (© 2016), *I Saw an Invisible Lion Today: Quatrains* (© 2016), and *Underneath My Bed: List Poems* (© 2017).

Some illustrations by Andy Rowland included in this volume were previously published in *If It Rains Pancakes: Haiku and Lantern Poems* (© 2014), *Ode to a Commode: Concrete Poems* (© 2015), *Something Sure Smells Around Here: Limericks* (© 2015), and *Bow-Tie Pasta: Acrostic Poems* (© 2016).

Additional illustrations by Richard Watson included in this volume were previously published in *I Saw an Invisible Lion Today: Quatrains* (© 2016) and *Underneath My Bed: List Poems* (© 2017).

Millbrook Press™
An imprint of Lerner Publishing Group, Inc.
241 First Avenue North
Minneapolis, MN 55401 USA

For reading levels and more information, look up this title at www.lernerbooks.com.

Designed by Emily Harris.
Main body text set in Avenir LT Std. Typeface provided by Adobe Systems.

Library of Congress Cataloging-in-Publication Data

Names: Cleary, Brian P., 1959– author. | Rowland, Andy, 1962– illustrator.
Title: Eating my words : and 128 other poems / Brian P. Cleary ; illustrated by Andy Rowland.
Other titles: Eating my words (Compilation)
Description: Minneapolis : Millbrook Press, 2024. | Includes glossary of poetic terms. | Audience: Ages 9–14. | Audience: Grades 4–6. | Summary: "A playful and punny illustrated poetry collection from Brian Cleary that's perfect for middle grade readers. Includes quick tips about poetic forms and poetic devices that teachers can use in poetry lessons" —Provided by publisher.
Identifiers: LCCN 2023029960 (print) | LCCN 2023029961 (ebook) | ISBN 9781728487649 (library binding) | ISBN 9798765625194 (paperback) | ISBN 9798765619223 (epub)
Subjects: LCSH: Children's poetry, American. | Humorous poetry, American. | Poetry—History and criticism—Juvenile literature. | CYAC: American poetry. | Humorous poetry. | Poetry—History and criticism. | BISAC: JUVENILE NONFICTION / Poetry / Humorous | LCGFT: Humorous poetry. | Literary criticism.
Classification: LCC PS3553.L39144 E18 2024 (print) | LCC PS3553.L39144 (ebook) | DDC 811/.54—dc23/eng/20230803

LC record available at https://lccn.loc.gov/2023029960
LC ebook record available at https://lccn.loc.gov/2023029961

Manufactured in the United States of America
1-52909-51005-10/24/2023

Brian P. Cleary

EATING MY  WORDS

AND 128 OTHER POEMS

illustrations by **Andy Rowland**
and **Richard Watson**

M MILLBROOK PRESS · MINNEAPOLIS

CONTENTS

INTRODUCTION 6

THERE ONCE WAS A STUDENT NAMED SONNY .. 8

SAID LITTLE FIRST GRADER PAM PLUNKETT 8

A GREAT PASTA MAKER NAMED FREDDY 9

MY LAPTOP, WITH SKILL AND FINESSE 9

AT THE BUS STOP 10

THE JOY OF DISCOVERY 11

I CAN'T FIND MY THESAURUS 12

ROBERT TREBOR 13

TRICERATOPS 14

PIANO 15

MY THREE DOGS 16

WHERE HOME IS 17

LESSON LEARNED 17

GOING UP 18

ODE TO A COMMODE 19

SPRING 20

BUS 20

ZZZZZZZZ 21

GOTCHA 21

PUN WITH GRANDMA AND GRANDPA 22

HAVING PUN WITH MY FRIENDS 23

VERY SCARY 24

SPANISH LESSONS (EASY AS 1, 2, 3) 25

SYL-LA-BLES 25

EARLY ONE MOTHER'S DAY, JAKE 26

A FROG DROVE HER CAR DOWN THE ROAD 27

I MET A YOUNG SPIDER NAMED DEB 27

GREAT-GRANDMOTHER'S PET STORE 28

YELLOW 29

IT'S RAINING ADJECTIVES 30

RAINY DAY 32

POEM 33

WINTER 33

WE'RE GOING TO THE VILLA, NELL 34

JUMP ROPE SONG 35

HORIZON 36

NO QUESTION, MARK 37

REVERSAL 38

APRIL 38

NATURE 39

COLOR ME CONFUSED 39

HOW MANY BIRDS MAKE A PUN? 40

HAVING PUN WITH THE FAMILY 40

EATING MY WORDS 41

MY BEAUTIFUL VOICE 42

THE GAG BAG 43

"AHOY!" SAID A PIRATE NAMED MARRRRTY 44

A MAN ON A BUS IN MANHATTAN 45

THE SCHOOL MICROWAVE 46

I'VE DONE (ALMOST) EVERYTHING 48

AT THE MUZZALOO STORE 49

TEACHERS 50

SHARKS 51

PENCIL 51

THE "I-KNOW-WHAT'S-AILIN'-ME" BLUES 52

SPORTING KIDS 53

TENNIS BALL 54

THE GIRAFFE 55

YUMMY 56

THE MIND 56

HAIKU 57

WHAT I'D DO IF A BURGLAR

BROKE INTO MY HOUSE* 58

I'LL LOVE YOU TILL THE BUTTERFLIES 58

DELIVER ME 59

A LIMERICK POET, MS. SHEETS 60

MOM SAID THAT OUR DOG'S

PART RETRIEVER 60

THE C@ WAS OUT OF H& 61

NO WONDER 62

COME APRIL 63

WHEN I AM NO LONGER 64

ON OPPOSITE DAY 65

GIGGLE 66

JOKES 67

SPIDER 67

STOP AWHILE 68

BIKING, MACKENZIE ONCE RODE 70

A TALENTED STUDENT NAMED HALEY 70

THE TRUMPET 71

GOING GREEN 72

THE GLOVE COMPARTMENT OF OUR VAN 73

IT'S GRANDMA 74

THERE'S A REASON I'M ASKING 75

BANANAS 75

RELATIVELY SPEAKING 76

TO E. E. CUMMINGS 77

SLEEPOVER PARTY 78

I BABYSAT (ONCE) 79

AT SUMMER CAMP 80

WHERE I'M FROM 81

IT COULD BE WORSE 82

QUADRUPLICATES 82

HOME 83

MY BROTHER JOE 84

MAKING RIPPLES 85

JOY 86

STORY PROBLEM 86

TRANSLATION 87

IN THE POCKETS OF MY CARGO SHORTS 88

LOVE AND PEACE 89

YOU'RE SUPPOSED TO BE YOU 90

AT THE SHORE 91

I WISH I HAD MY BIRTHDAY
TEN TIMES YEARLY 92

THE DAY THE COMMAS CALLED IN SICK 93

FORTY 93

HOW TO WRITE A COW POEM 94

GRANDPA'S HANDS 95

OUR ALPHABETICAL CLASSROOM 96

MY CAT BYTES 98

MIXED MARRIAGE 99

NOSE FLOOD 99

MY BEAGLE'S BREATH SMELLS
NOTHING LIKE A ROSE 100

IF I COULD DUNK A BASKETBALL 101

I'VE GOT YOUR NUMBER 102

DEAD TO ME 102

IT'S PRETTY SIMPLE 103

IN A FIX 104

MY FATHER'S MUSTACHE 106

FIVE 106

MAKE A WISH 107

MS. GARCIA AND ONOMATOPOEIA 108

I SPOTTED A LEOPARD 109

SNOW DAY 109

SCENES FROM THE HALLWAY 110

MY DREAM IN RHYME 111

IT'S COMPLICATED 112

CAN'T WAIT TILL NEXT YEAR 113

CAT-ATONIC 114

A RECIPE FOR POETRY 115

GLOSSARY OF POETIC TERMS 116

FURTHER READING 119

INDEX OF POETIC FORMS 120

INTRODUCTION

The universe has a rhythm to it. You don't have to retreat to some silent place to access it. This pulse—this *beat*—is evident, not just in the ocean lapping the shore or the wind in the trees but also in the chug of a train, the patter of rain on a window, or even the percussion of the garbage truck wheezing to a stop every forty feet on your street.

I like to think of that pulse as the world's heartbeat. There are more than seven thousand languages, and all of them have poetry. While the poetic forms might differ from language to language, culture to culture, poems serve a similar purpose: to reveal truth, spark joy, help us understand others, and make some kind of a comment on what it means to be human. Thousands of languages but one heartbeat.

I've enjoyed language, wordplay, jokes, and rhyme ever since I was a young child. While other students were dreaming of being a rock star, an astronaut, or a pro athlete, I was perfecting my autograph for when I inevitably became an author. My mom and dad bought me a rhyming dictionary for my eighth birthday, and they never gave me any reason to doubt that I'd write books when the time came. I still use it to this day.

I believe that reading and writing poetry not only connects us to the billions of other humans who make up our planet but also to the universe itself, as we interpret the stars that wink, breezes that whisper, and lightning that dances across the sky. And poetry isn't just a spectator sport, so go ahead—read, write, and share!

There once was a student named Sonny
who bought books of jokes with his money.
He ate one at lunchtime,
then gave as his punch line,
"That tasted a little bit funny."

rhyme scheme *AABBA*

Said little first grader Pam Plunkett,
"The past tense of 'shrink it' is 'shrunk it.'"
Told, "Yes, that is true!
Just who taught that to you?"
she said, "Not really sure, I just thunk it."

rhyme scheme *AABBA*

A great pasta maker named Freddy
cooked eight hundred pounds of spaghetti.
He carted it down
to the center of town,
rang a bell, and then yelled, "Supper's ready!"

rhyme scheme *AABBA*

My laptop, with skill and finesse,
has a brain that can beat me at chess.
But with no arms or body,
it stinks at karate.
Now please help me clean up this mess.

rhyme *scheme AABBA*

> Limericks are often funny five-line poems that were popularized
> by English artist and poet Edward Lear. Lines 1, 2, and 5 rhyme
> with one another, and lines 3 and 4 are shorter and rhyme with
> each other, but not the other three lines.

AT THE BUS STOP

Jennifer jumps rope.

Tonya texts.

Tony twirls like a ballerina.

Hailey hums.

William whistles.

Chloe catches up on reading.

Luke listens to tunes.

Miles munches.

Peyton plays I spy.

Jackson jokes.

Logan laughs.

Shawn shows Cheyenne the green, scaly, slimy bug he
      found in his bed this morning.

This poem features lots of alliteration (repetition of the same sound—often the same letter—in the beginning of words that are near one another) and consonance (the repetition of similar sounds, especially consonants, in any part of words that are near one another).

List poems, as the name suggests, are made up of lists of things, places, people, colors, emotions, sounds, events, and more. Some rhyme and some don't, and they can make you think, smile, squirm, giggle, nod your head, or sigh.

THE JOY OF DISCOVERY

Each week, I'm asked to clean my room, but what I do instead
is simply take the whole week's mess to stash beneath my bed.
Then came the day I didn't have a single thing to wear
or read or dry myself with, so I took a look down there.
I found two books, three towels, some long-thought lost remotes,
cereal and sunscreen and two fall-and-winter coats,
pizza crust, some pants and shirts, some shorts and underpants,
socks and shoes, a sticky, swirly sucker . . . and some ants.

rhyme scheme *AABBCCDD*

I CAN'T FIND MY THESAURUS

I can't find my thesaurus.
I'm really quite disturbed,
aggravated, agitated,
angry, and perturbed.

Whoever came and borrowed it:
return it straightaway,
instantly, directly—
right this minute! Now!! Today!!!

rhyme scheme *ABCB DEFE*

> A quatrain is a four-line verse that usually rhymes. It could
> be just one stanza (like a paragraph of poetry) in a longer
> poem or the entire poem. Quatrains come in more than ten
> possible rhyme schemes or patterns.

ROBERT TREBOR

Since Robert Trebor learned to spell,
he's always loved his name.
'Cause if you write it left or right,
it comes out just the same.

He yells it to the canyons,
and he sings it to the blackbirds.
"My name is so amazing,
you can say it front or backwards!"

rhyme scheme *ABCB DEFE*

Words or phrases that are spelled the same way backward and forward are called palindromes. A palindrome can be a phrase like "a Toyota," a word like "kayak," a name like "Hannah," or even a number like "747."

Two hard horns and a third soft one that's

Really a snout made from soft proteins.

Inside its mouth: 200 to 800 teeth.

Can you imagine the dentist appointments?

Extinct, so none are living.

Rumored to be a slow walker.

Ate only plants.

T. rex wanted to have it for lunch.

Older than your parents and even your teacher!

Popular in dinosaur movies.

Seen last alive: 65 million years ago.

Parading down Main Street,

Is a sea of red-uniformed players of flute

And clarinet and drum,

Navigating their way through confetti and applause.

Only wish that I could march with my instrument.

An acrostic poem is a written piece in which a particular set of letters—most often the first letter of each line—spells out a word or phrase. The word or phrase it spells out is called the acrostich, and it is usually the subject of the piece.

MY THREE DOGS

My dog Moxie runs like the rain,
growls like a lion,
and soars like a plane.

My dog Izzy is bright as a star,
soft as a pillowcase,
fast as a car.

My dog Bailiff is as big as a mountain,
as slow as erosion,
and squirts like a fountain.

rhyme scheme *ABA CDC* . . .

Similes compare two unlike things (such as your mom and an ox) using the words "like" or "as." "My mom is strong as an ox," is an example of a simile. Can you find the similes in this poem?

WHERE HOME IS

Where I smell my dad's morning coffee,
my mom's meatballs,
and my grandma's lotion—
that's where home is.

Naani is an Indian form of poetry. It has four lines,
a total of between twenty and twenty-five syllables,
and is often about relationships.

LESSON LEARNED

Celebrating
an athletic win?
Tossing the ball
triumphantly
into the crowd of spectators
works better
in football,
than,
say,
bowling.

Enjambment is the continuation of a sentence from one line or stanza of a poem
to the next. The words "run over" or "spill over" from one line to the next.
Lines without enjambment are called end-stopped.

GOING UP

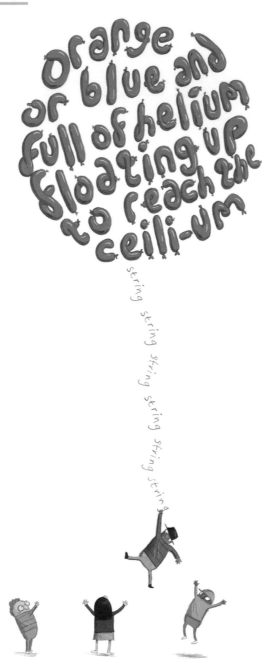

Orange or blue and full of helium floating up to reach the ceili-um

string string string string string string

rhyme scheme *AA*

ODE TO A COMMODE

Flush goes the sound of the toilet! The water (with everything in it) vanishes in a swirl and a whoosh, and the bowl fills back up in a minute!

rhyme scheme *AA*

A concrete poem's shape resembles the subject of the poem. The letters, words, or symbols are arranged on the page to make a picture.

Spring.
Yellows,
blues, and greens.
Chirp, peck, peep, pop,
bloom.

Bus
wheezes
to a stop.
Doors gasp open.
Home!

A lantern (sometimes spelled lanturne or lanterne) poem is a short Japanese form of poetry. Line 1 consists of a one-syllable noun (person, place, or thing). That noun is the subject of the poem. The following lines describe that subject—or as the name *lantern* suggests, *shed light* on it. Line 2 has two syllables. Line 3 has three syllables. Line 4 has four. Line 5 goes back to one syllable. All lines are centered on the page, so the finished poem roughly resembles the shape of a Japanese lantern.

ZZZZZZZZ

On the other side
of the pillow—that's where all
the best dreams are found.

GOTCHA

What I if told you
that you read the poem's first line
erroneously?

A haiku has three lines. Line 1 has five syllables, line 2 has seven, and the final line has five. Think of a haiku as a sandwich, with the five-syllable lines as the bread and the seven-syllable line as the stuff in the middle. Traditionally, haiku have nature as their subject.

PUN WITH GRANDMA AND GRANDPA

When we GOPHER fishing trips,
my grandpa YAKS till dawn.
"My fishing isn't bad," he says,
"but, man, my HERRING's gone!"

My grandma wears a two-foot wig
that's held on with APE pin.
But if you think her HARE is big,
EWE OTTER SEA URCHIN.

Although she's funny looking,
she's DEER as she can be.
When once I asked her for some DOE,
she gave a BUCK to me.

rhyme scheme *ABCB DEDE FGHG*

EATING MY WORDS • BRIAN P. CLEARY

HAVING PUN WITH MY FRIENDS

My Buddy, Bert, likes HAYDN things—
he's sometimes hard to HANDEL.
I said, "Give me BACH my SCHUBERT,"
'cause I knew he hid my sandal.

My friends the twins look so alike
that some CHIMES I forget—
I often think Annette is Claire,
or I'll call CLARINET.

The crossing guard has warned us:
"There could be A MAJOR loss,
'cause if you don't C-SHARP, you could
B-FLAT before you cross!"

rhyme scheme *ABCB DEFE* . . .

A pun is a verbal joke or play on words that uses words or phrases
with multiple meanings, often with a humorous result.

VERY SCARY

Doors that creak while I'm in bed,
the vacant house beside us,
a story of a ghoul or ghost,
our neighbor's pit bull, Midas.
The big, black crow upon the post
with eyes as dark as toffee—
none is half as frightening
as Mom before her coffee.

rhyme scheme *ABCBDEFE*

Feminine rhyme is a rhyme of two or more syllables in which the first syllable is the strongest, such as "toffee" and "coffee."

Trochaic refers to a poetic meter pattern that begins with a stressed, or emphasized, syllable followed by an unstressed, or softer, syllable. Example: Brian (BRI-an) has one stressed syllable followed by one that is unstressed.

SPANISH LESSONS (EASY AS 1, 2, 3)

U-NO! A spider's on my nose!
It's something I must face.
I'd like a DOS of courage,
But I haven't got a TRES.

rhyme scheme *ABCB*

Macaronic verses are rhyming poems that include words from other languages. What English words do the capitalized Spanish words sound like?

SYL-LA-BLES

A name such as Julia
often will fulia.
Is it two beats or three?

Beats me.

rhyme scheme *AABB*

A syllable is a part of a word that has a single vowel sound and is pronounced in one beat. So for example, "play" has one syllable and "playground" has two.

Early one Mother's Day, Jake
decided that he'd like to bake
a pie for his mother,
but soon he'd discover
it surely was no piece of cake.

rhyme scheme *AABBA*

Limericks are often funny five-line poems that were popularized
by English artist and poet Edward Lear. Lines 1, 2, and 5 rhyme
with one another, and lines 3 and 4 are shorter and rhyme with
each other, but not the other three lines.

A frog drove her car down the road.
Hearing one of her tires explode,
the frog didn't panic—
she called her mechanic,
and next thing you know, she was *toad*.

rhyme scheme *AABBA*

I met a young spider named Deb
who's become quite a singing celeb.
When I asked how she'd grown
to be so well known,
she replied, "I'm all over the web!"

rhyme scheme *AABBA*

GREAT-GRANDMOTHER'S PET STORE

Great-grandmother ran a popular shop,
according to Grandma and Daddy.
Customers came from all over the state
to her pet store in south Cincinnati.

She had chickens, Chihuahuas, chinchillas, and chipmunks,
greyhounds and geckos and geese,
pelicans, poodles, and panthers . . . plus parrots,
(which sold for a dollar apiece!).

Kangaroos, kittens, koalas, and kiwis
would play on the shop's second floor.
It's always such fun to hear Grandma and Daddy
tell tales of Great-Grandmother's store.

rhyme scheme *ABCB DEFE* . . .

YELLOW

Butterscotch and bumblebees,
ears of corn and mac and cheese,
pet canaries, dandelions,
those silly shoes of Uncle Brian's,
scrambled eggs and globs of mustard,
caution signs, banana custard.
smiley faces, butterflies,
rubber chickens, lemon pies,
an ancient book that you might read,
the snow right where a dog just peed,
a daffodil, the stars and sun—
oops, my cab's here—gotta run!

rhyme scheme *AABBCCDD* . . .

List poems, as the name suggests, are made up of lists of things, places, people, colors, emotions, sounds, events, and more. Some rhyme and some don't, and they can make you think, smile, squirm, giggle, nod your head, or sigh.

IT'S RAINING ADJECTIVES

Hey, look! It's raining adjectives!
It's pouring plain and fancy.
It's dripping dark and dangerous,
mysterious and chancy.

My hat is drenched in jubilant.
The puddles pop with jumpy.
My socks are soaked with squishy, smelly,
soggy, soft, and lumpy.

The gutter's overflowing too
with spooky, strange, and sneaky.
The drain is backing up with loaded,
laughable, and leaky.

It's coming down with clamorous,
cantankerous, and clunky.
It's splattering, splendiferous,
fantabulous, and funky.

The weatherman looks skyward,
as he shouts, "What's up? What gives?
It isn't raining cats and dogs—
it's raining adjectives!"

rhyme scheme *ABCB DEFE . . .*

This poem features lots of alliteration (repetition of the same sound—often the same letter—in the beginning of words that are near one another) and consonance (the repetition of similar sounds, especially consonants, in any part of words that are near one another).

A quatrain is a four-line verse that usually rhymes. It could be just one stanza (like a paragraph of poetry) in a longer poem or the entire poem. Quatrains come in more than ten possible rhyme schemes or patterns.

Reading in a cozy nook.
Asking for another book.
I make cookies by the sheet.
Next, they cool. I dunk, then eat.
Yo-yo, board games, watch the rain,
Draw a face inside each pane.
Afterward, I make some s'mores.
Yes, I love the great indoors!

rhyme scheme *AABBCCDD*

An acrostic poem is a written piece in which a particular set of letters—most often the first letter of each line—spells out a word or phrase. The word or phrase it spells out is called the acrostich, and it is usually the subject of the piece.

Poppies are red.
Orchids are blue.
Ever try to rhyme stuff?
Man, it's really hard.

Wind whipping white little swirls of snow.
Icicles are reaching to the drifts that grow below.
Night is falling early, and dawn is sleeping in.
Time for cocoa from a cup and cookies from a tin.
Extra-toasty blankets on an extra-cozy bed,
Rosy cheeks and frosty peaks and riding on a sled.

rhyme scheme *AABBCC*

Personification is what we call giving human qualities to a nonliving object, such as a bus or a guitar. Examples: "The sky cried" and "the bus wheezed to a stop."

WE'RE GOING TO THE VILLA, NELL

School is over, sounds the bell,
and that means summer has begun.
We're going to the villa, Nell.

Where we'll catch toads and mackerel
and swim all day beneath the sun.
School is over, sounds the bell.

The voice of our Aunt Isabel
will blend with Dad's accordion.
We're going to the villa, Nell.

Where watermelon twilights fell
since we were two and one.
School is over, sounds the bell.

I'll race you to the old stone well,
and Mom can say which one has won.
We're going to the villa, Nell.

"It's snowing fireflies," you'll yell,
as crickets croon and rapids run.
School is over, sounds the bell.
We're going to the villa, Nell.

rhyme scheme *ABA ABA ABA ABA ABA ABAA*

> A villanelle is a French form of poetry that is nineteen lines long. Line 1 is repeated on lines 6, 12, and 18. Line 3 is repeated on lines 9, 15, and 19. The second line of each stanza rhymes all the way through the poem. Once you've written lines 1 and 3, you are almost halfway done! Did you find the pun in this poem?

JUMP ROPE SONG

Popcorn, pizza, watermelon pie.
Bug juice, baseball,
skeeter on your thigh.

Kickball, kickstand, sleepin' on the roof.
Molly has a collie
and he goes "woof, woof!"

Brother's on the back porch,
sister's on the swing.
Mama's in the maple tree a-waitin' for the spring.

Baby's in the buggy,
Daddy's in the den.
But we all get together when we count to ten . . .

rhyme scheme *ABA CDC EFF GHH*

Jump rope rhymes or skipping rope rhymes are hundreds of years old. The rhythm of the jump rope's rotation is synced to the rhythm or the beat of the rhymed verse. This "marriage" of rhyming or chanting while jumping rope can be seen in many cultures around the world.

HORIZON

outintheeastwherethesunisarisin',there'salinejustlikethis,andit'scalledahorizon.

rhyme scheme *AA*

NO QUESTION, MARK

"I wonder," said Mark, "if this big brown dog has a bite that lives up to its bark." If you'd like to know, you can question the dog, but there's no way to question Mark.

rhyme scheme *AA*

A concrete poem's shape resembles the subject of the poem. The letters, words, or symbols are arranged on the page to make a picture.

REVERSAL

Noses smell. Feet run.
But the opposite also
is oftentimes true.

APRIL

Yellow tulips rise
as if they're awakening
from winter's slumber.

A haiku has three lines. Line 1 has five syllables, line 2 has seven, and the final line has five. Think of a haiku as a sandwich, with the five-syllable lines as the bread and the seven-syllable line as the stuff in the middle. Traditionally, haiku have nature as their subject.

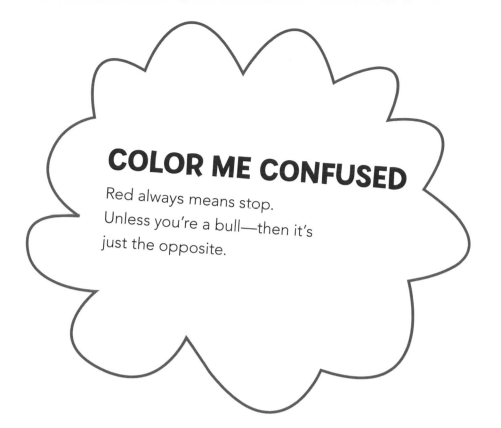

COLOR ME CONFUSED

Red always means stop.
Unless you're a bull—then it's
just the opposite.

NATURE

Brown leaves, curled and dried.
Acorns, straw, and rich, brown dirt.
I should clean my room.

HOW MANY BIRDS MAKE A PUN?

If you want to disagree with me, then go ahead, you can . . .
while one bird cannot make a pun, it seems somehow, toucan.

rhyme scheme *AA*

> A couplet consists of two lines of verse that typically have the same meter and rhyme at the end.

HAVING PUN WITH THE FAMILY

Aunt Anna can fix anything—
a PARIS skates, a cup.
If your pants rip INDONESIA
just HAVANA sew 'em up!

My dad comes home so tired,
he can't keep his BERING STRAIT.
His SUDAN THAILAND on the floor,
his shoes land on his plate.

He took me to the racetrack.
KENYA tell why I'm upset?
I picked out all the winners,
but he's just too cheap TIBET!

rhyme scheme *ABCB DEFE* . . .

> A pun is a verbal joke or play on words that uses words or phrases with multiple meanings, often with a humorous result.

EATING MY WORDS

At lunch,
I ate three cans
of alphabet soup.
An hour later,
I had
thesaurus
throat
ever.

Free verse is a form of
poetry that does not rhyme
or have a regular meter to it.

Did you notice there is also
a pun in this poem?

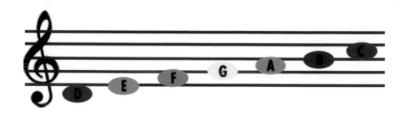

Musicians use these symbols and lines to represent notes on what they call a staff. The treble clef at the beginning lets them know which line or space represents which note. By using this key, you can decode the little musical puzzles that will help you spell the words that are missing from the poems. Each of the notes corresponds to a letter, which will help you turn these lines and dots into words!

MY BEAUTIFUL VOICE

I had a little hamster I kept beside my

I sang to him each night until the day I found him

Inside the  , he lay so still, I cried to Mom and Dad,

I just had no idea that my singing was so

rhyme scheme *AABB*

THE GAG BAG

At Halloween, my 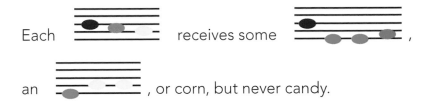 will never hand out gum or sweets.

Each trick-or-treater's [music notation] just falls when first they see our "treats."

Each [music notation] receives some [music notation], an [music notation], or corn, but never candy.

"Whatever's in the fridge," he'll [music notation], "whatever food is handy."

Each Halloween it's been the same,

no matter how we've [music notation].

It's been at least a 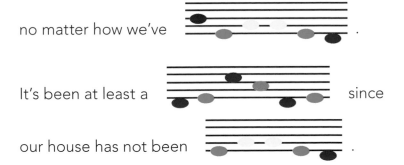 since

our house has not been [music notation].

rhyme scheme ABCBDEFE . . .

"Ahoy!" said a pirate named MARRRRty,
who was fun loving, healthy, and hEARRRRRty.
"I believe it's my duty
to go shake my booty,
'cause nothin's more fun than a pARRRRRty!"

rhyme scheme *AABBA*

On the acres of Old Farmer Akkers,
you'll find there's no hay, no wheat stackers,
no pigpens, no plows—
only ducklings and cows.
He calls his place "Just Milk and Quackers."

rhyme scheme *AABBA*

A man on a bus in Manhattan
was fluent in German and Latin.
Though he could speak either,
we found he used neither
when he looked down and saw what he sat in.

rhyme scheme *AABBA*

Limericks are often funny five-line poems that were popularized by English artist and poet Edward Lear. Lines 1, 2, and 5 rhyme with one another, and lines 3 and 4 are shorter and rhyme with each other, but not the other three lines.

THE SCHOOL MICROWAVE

The microwave at school is gross;
it has the caked remains
of stuff that looks a bit like blood
and scabs and parts of brains.

You see the crumbs from fish sticks
and the sauce from fettuccine.
The noodle types found there include
spaghetti and linguine.

Iambic refers to a poetic meter pattern
that begins with an unstressed syllable
followed by a stressed, or stronger, syllable.
Example: the word *vanilla* (va-NIL-la).
That's an unstressed syllable followed by a
stressed, or stronger, one.

EATING MY WORDS • BRIAN P. CLEARY

Nachos? Cocoa? Tenders?
You'll find signs of each of these
along with chicken patties, eggs,
and several kinds of cheese.

With hardened broth and hot dog juice,
the sides are brown and rough.
But whatever I heat up in there
tastes like my favorite stuff!

rhyme scheme *ABCB DEFE* . . .

List poems, as the name suggests,
are made up of lists of things,
places, people, colors, emotions,
sounds, events, and more. Some
rhyme and some don't, and they
can make you think, smile, squirm,
giggle, nod your head, or sigh.

I'VE DONE (ALMOST) EVERYTHING

I speak about a dozen different languages.
I've won all thirteen marathons I've run.
I've written several superhero comic books,
invented both the hot dog and the bun.

I coined the phrase, "What's up?" when I was seven.
I once flew back in time to see Babe Ruth.
I struck him out with three—yes, it's amazing being me.
I've done everything, except, well . . . tell the truth.

rhyme scheme *ABCB DEFE*

Masculine rhyme occurs when the rhyming words either have one syllable (example: "Ruth" and "truth") or when the rhyme is in the final syllable of a multisyllable word or phrase ("direct" and "respect" or "to sleep" and "to sweep").

A quatrain is a four-line verse that usually rhymes. It could be just one stanza (like a paragraph of poetry) in a longer poem or the entire poem. Quatrains come in more than ten possible rhyme schemes or patterns.

AT THE MUZZALOO STORE

At the muzzaloo store, there are crates of persnoobles,
fresh-baked flobitzen, and tazbees with jubles.
They're stocking the shelves with the best alaprises,
Ungden, and traffadoo (three different sizes!).

High on the shelf, you'll find mezeloid dinkles—
the nice, silky, smooth kind without any wrinkles.
Jars filled with tomashes and wazzenloft too.
Boxes of mooglehorns, yellow and blue.

Right down aisle seven is where they keep japers—
stacked and wrapped neatly in pink tissue papers—
mozenar, trums, castanoovas, and more:
you'll find all of these at the muzzaloo store!

rhyme scheme *AABB CCDD* . . .

This poem is both a quatrain
and a list poem.

They are the superheroes who show up
Each and every day, not just when some special signal or
Alarm is activated. They answer the call without
Costumes, without masks. Their
Headquarters? A classroom. Their mission?
Engaging and inspiring students.
Rescuing them from boredom, they light the flame of curiosity,
Saving more lives than all those cape-wearing showoffs combined.

An acrostic poem is a written piece in which a particular set of letters—most often the first letter of each line—spells out a word or phrase. The word or phrase it spells out is called the acrostich, and it is usually the subject of the piece.

Skeletons made of flexible cartilage.
Have multiple rows of teeth.
Active at night, when looking for food.
Really keen sense of smell.
Known to have existed before dinosaurs.
Silly question to ask one: "Wanna go swimming?"

Point: all worn down,
Eraser: black and flat,
Nasty teeth marks,
Chipped, yellow paint,
Inch-and-a-half long.
Lots of good words left in it.

THE "I-KNOW-WHAT'S-AILIN'-ME" BLUES

I ain't got no measles on me.
I ain't got no measles on me.
I ain't got no measles as you can plainly see.
I ain't got no measles on me.

I ain't got no strep throat in me.
I ain't got no strep throat in me.
I ain't got no strep throat said Ol' Doc MacAvee.
I ain't got no strep throat in me.

Ain't got no bronchitis in me.
Ain't got no bronchitis in me.
Ain't got no bronchitis, arthritis, or bursitis.
Ain't got no bronchitis in me.

Doc says ain't nothing wrong with me.
Doc says ain't nothing wrong with me.
In his vestibule today,
he sent me back to school today.
Doc says ain't nothing wrong with me.

rhyme scheme *AAAA* for stanzas 1 and 2; *AABA* for stanza 3; *AACCA* for stanza 4

> The blues is an African American musical art form. The first and second lines in each verse are typically identical, and the subject of the song usually has to do with something that makes the singer sad or "blue."

SPORTING KIDS

Soccer kids are such a kick—they always have a ball.
Hockey kids are oh so cool, especially when they fall.
Baseball kids will sacrifice to help their teammate score.
And kids whose game is basketball? They dribble on the floor.
Football kids are in a rush to end up on the ground.
And the alleys and the gutters are where bowling kids are found.
A stroke is good for swimming kids, and golfing kids as well.
But kids who run cross-country? Why, they just run like . . .
heck!

rhyme scheme *AABBCCDE*

If you follow the rhyme scheme here, does the ending surprise you at all?

A couplet consists of two lines of verse that typically have the same meter and rhyme at the end.

TENNIS BALL

Tennis ball,
.llaw eht ffo

rhyme scheme *AA*

A concrete poem's shape resembles the subject of the poem. The letters, words, or symbols are arranged on the page to make a picture.

EATING MY WORDS • BRIAN P. CLEARY

THE GIRAFFE

The giraffe is a creature with an interesting feature. He's unlike a camel or goat. So lengthy is he that he dines from a tree, but—OUCH—when he gets a sore throat!

rhyme scheme *AABCCB*

YUMMY

When something's so good
you want to taste it again,
that's what burps are for.

THE MIND

Memory is like
a room where tiny boxes
hold our yesterdays.

HAIKU

When you've written one
without enough syllables,
you add words. Football.

A haiku has three lines. Line 1 has five syllables, line 2 has seven, and the final line has five. Think of a haiku as a sandwich, with the five-syllable lines as the bread and the seven-syllable line as the stuff in the middle. Traditionally, haiku have nature as their subject.

WHAT I'D DO IF A BURGLAR BROKE INTO MY HOUSE*

I'd
hide.

rhyme scheme *AA*

*At six letters, this is believed to be the shortest poem ever.

I'LL LOVE YOU TILL THE BUTTERFLIES

I'll love you till the BUTTERFLIES,
until the SUGAR BOWLS.
I'll love you till the KITCHEN SINKS,
and CELERY STALKS the rolls.

rhyme scheme *ABCB*

> Wordplay is a device that lyricists and poets use to form a funny piece of writing. Wordplay might employ puns, rhyme, alliteration, and other literary tools for comic effect.

DELIVER ME

I like pizza when I wake, not eggs or toast or coffee cake.
I like pizza in my lunch. After school it's great to munch.

I like pizza in the mall, in a restaurant, house, or hall.
I like pizza for dessert. I've even licked it off my shirt.

I like pizza by the sheet, filled with sauce and cheese and meat.
I like pizza by the slice, from any place at any price.

Sausage, peppers, double cheese, everything but anchovies.
Pepperoni, even chicken—all these get my lips a lickin'.

I like pizza hot or cold, nice and fresh or three days old.
And though I'd like to tell you more—the pizza guy is at my door.

rhyme scheme *AA BB CC DD*

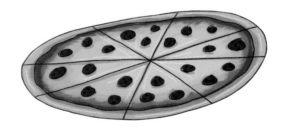

This poem uses a device called internal rhyme. (Did you notice "wake" rhymes with "cake" in line 1?)

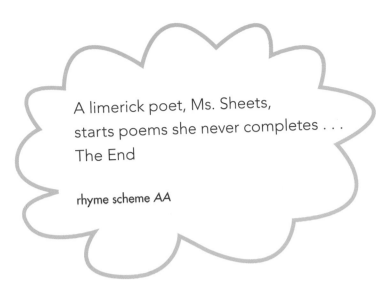

A limerick poet, Ms. Sheets,
starts poems she never completes . . .
The End

rhyme scheme *AA*

Mom said that our dog's part retriever,
part collie, part badger and beaver,
and part German shepherd,
part penguin, part leopard.
I'm not sure if I should believe her.

rhyme scheme *AABBA*

THE C@ WAS OUT OF H&

A sleepwalking calico c@
some days walks away from her m@.
She strolls all about
the city without
having even a clue where she's @.

One evening, completely unpl&,
she walked to a tavern to st&
at the bar on this outing,
and was heard to be shouting,
"I can lick any c@ in the l&."

rhyme scheme *AABBA CCDDC*

Having trouble figuring this one out? Just sound out the letters before the signs for "at" and "and." See how it reads? How many other words could you come up with like these? Also, can "lick" have two meanings? This poem is basically a double limerick in terms of form.

Limericks are often funny five-line poems that were popularized by English artist and poet Edward Lear. Lines 1, 2, and 5 rhyme with one another, and lines 3 and 4 are shorter and rhyme with each other, but not the other three lines.

NO WONDER

Stegosauruses
had no skateboards,
no electronic tablets,
no Coca-Cola,
no gaming consoles,
no bubble gum,
no TV,
no internet,
no pizza,
no basketballs,
no ice cream,
no smartphones,
no bicycles,
no french fries,
no amusement parks,
and
no Oreos.
. . . and we wonder why they didn't survive.

COME APRIL

Come April,
windows open.
Baseballs fly.
The birds go cheep, cheep, cheep.
Bunnies hop.
Rain falls.
And crocuses sing to the heavens.

List poems, as the name suggests, are made up of lists of things, places, people, colors, emotions, sounds, events, and more. Some rhyme and some don't, and they can make you think, smile, squirm, giggle, nod your head, or sigh.

WHEN I AM NO LONGER

They can give my arms to the army,
take my eyes of blue,
and give my knees to the needy,
but my heart goes out to you.

My ears will go to the eerie—
it's scary, but it's true.
The rest can go to science,
but my heart goes out to you.

They'll give my nose to the nosy,
my toes to a tow truck too.
They'll give my hands to a handyman,
but my heart goes out to you.

They can take my shins to a shindig,
to the hip, my hips impart.
You can give my wrists to a 'ristocrat,
but it's you who gets my heart.

rhyme scheme *ABCB DBEB FBGB HIJI*

> Wordplay is a device that lyricists and poets use to form a funny piece of writing. Wordplay might employ puns, rhyme, alliteration, and other literary tools for comic effect.

> A quatrain is a four-line verse that usually rhymes. It could be just one stanza (like a paragraph of poetry) in a longer poem, or the entire poem. Quatrains come in more than ten possible rhyme schemes or patterns.

ON OPPOSITE DAY

On opposite day when up is down
and organized is messy,
off means on and in means out
and casual is dressy.

On opposite day, cloudy might
just take the place of sunny.
Mean is used instead of nice
and serious for funny.

If on this day when happy's sad
and awesome means unbearable,
your mom makes you your favorite soup,
just slurp and say, "That's terrible."

rhyme scheme *ABCB DEFE* . . .

Girl walks into a library and gets
In line with the other kids who are
Going up to check out their books.
Girl, when it's her turn, says, "Small cheese pizza, please."
Librarian says sternly, "*This* is a library!" Then the girl,
Ever-so-softly *whispers*, "Sorry . . . small cheese pizza, please."

An acrostic poem is a written piece in which a particular set of letters—most often the first letter of each line—spells out a word or phrase. The word or phrase it spells out is called the acrostich, and it is usually the subject of the piece.

Joe, an elephant, and
Olivia, a catfish, got married.
Know what she gave birth to
Eleven months after the wedding?
Swimming trunks.

Suspended in its silky web,
Positioned high in my bedroom's corner,
I want him gone but not
Dead. Armed with tissue and
Envelope, I nudge him from one to the other,
Relocating him to my sister's room.

STOP AWHILE

Geraldine, the Grammar Queen,
knows all about the comma—
she separates each phrase, as in,
your dad,
your sis,
your mama,
by dropping in the curly mark
to make us briefly pause.
Yes, Geraldine loves commas,
in a sentence, phrase, or clause.

Commas here,
commas there,
she just can't live without 'em.
She made a great big billboard
just to tell the town about 'em.
She put a ten-foot comma
on the billboard,
and she reckoned
that she could make the
traffic stop

if only for a second.*

rhyme scheme *ABCBDEFE* . . .

*Why would cars stop briefly when they saw a giant comma?

Line 1 of the first stanza uses a device called internal rhyme. (Did you notice "Geraldine" rhymes with "Queen"?)

Trochaic refers to a poetic meter pattern that begins with a stressed, or emphasized, syllable followed by an unstressed, or softer, syllable. Example: Brian (BRI-an) has one stressed syllable followed by one that is unstressed.

Biking, Mackenzie once rode
down a street—heard a "pop"—and she slowed.
In discovering that
her front tire was flat,
she said, "I just hit a fork in the road!"

rhyme scheme *AABBA*

A talented student named Haley
could play the French horn, ukulele,
the oboe, viola,
the drums, and mandola.
Her neighbors could vouch for that . . . daily.

rhyme scheme *AABBA*

EATING MY WORDS • BRIAN P. CLEARY

THE TRUMPET

The trumpet is loud, triumphant, and proud.
It's bold and incredibly brassy.
It can sound cool and shady,
behave like a lady,
or be guttural, gutsy, or classy.

The trumpet was born to blow its own horn.
It's been played both for princes and peasants.
The coronet's cousin,
with your lips a buzzin',
is ideal for announcing your presence!

rhyme scheme *ABCCB DEFFE*

Line 1 of each stanza uses a device called internal rhyme. (Did you notice "loud" rhymes with "proud" and "born" rhymes with "horn"?)

Feminine rhyme is a rhyme of two or more syllables in which the first syllable is the strongest, such as in brassy and classy.

Limericks are often funny five-line poems that were popularized by English artist and poet Edward Lear. Lines 1, 2, and 5 rhyme with one another, and lines 3 and 4 are shorter and rhyme with each other, but not the other three lines.

GOING GREEN

I've been dripping like a faucet from my nose for days and days—
ever since the day my allergies kicked in.
My phone is kind of sticky, and my doughnut has a glaze.
There's goop upon my shirt and violin.

I've got it on my locker, in my pencil case and books.
On my jacket, there's a green and shiny spot.
It's dotted both my socks and shoes—I get some crazy looks.
Don't tell me that it's funny . . . 'cause it's snot!

rhyme scheme *ABAB CDCD*

THE GLOVE COMPARTMENT OF OUR VAN

The glove compartment of our van
has napkins, gum, and maps,
sunglasses, a first-aid kit,
a pair of baseball caps,
old receipts and paperwork,
a flashlight and some mints,
a tiny thing of mouthwash
if somebody wants to rinse,
ketchup packets, tissues,
a lint brush and some wipes,
coupons, pen, a notepad
that has blue-and-yellow stripes.
The glove compartment of our van
has snacks my mother loves.
But the one thing that our glove compartment
doesn't have is . . . gloves.

rhyme scheme *ABCBDEFE* . . .

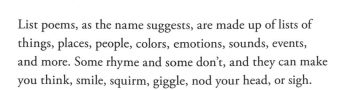

> List poems, as the name suggests, are made up of lists of
> things, places, people, colors, emotions, sounds, events,
> and more. Some rhyme and some don't, and they can make
> you think, smile, squirm, giggle, nod your head, or sigh.

IT'S GRANDMA

How to untangle a kinked-up hose?
Count to nineteen without using your toes?
Get pizza sauce out of your picture-day clothes?
You know who knows? Grandma knows.

Comes up with nicknames like Schnookems and Fuzz?
Knows the best lullaby there ever was?
Gives you a favorite treat . . . just because?
You know who does? Grandma does.

rhyme scheme *AAAA BBBB*

Trochaic refers to a poetic meter pattern that begins with a stressed, or emphasized, syllable followed by an unstressed, or softer, syllable. Example: Brian (BRI-an) has one stressed syllable, followed by one that is unstressed.

A quatrain is a four-line verse that usually rhymes. It could be just one stanza (like a paragraph of poetry) in a longer poem or the entire poem. Quatrains come in more than ten possible rhyme schemes or patterns.

EATING MY WORDS • BRIAN P. CLEARY

THERE'S A REASON I'M ASKING

What insect has eleven teeth,
is furry and oozing and black?
Has horns and a tail, some scabs underneath?
I don't know, but there's one on your back!

rhyme scheme *ABAB*

BANANAS

You're tasty and nutritious
in dessert or with a meal.
You come without a core or seeds
but always have a peel.

rhyme scheme *ABCB*

A pun is a verbal joke or play on words that uses words or phrases with multiple meanings, often with a humorous result.

RELATIVELY SPEAKING

Zadie's my dad's
second wife's second daughter,
and Teddy's my mother's first son.
He came from my mother's
first marriage to Terry
(although it was his second one).

Elaina's the offspring of Dad
and his first wife,
the one who would later elope
with one of Mom's exes—a doctor from Texas—
who always smelled strongly of soap.

There surely are twists in the trunk and the branches
that make up our family tree.
And though it's bemusing,
complex, and confusing,
without 'em we wouldn't have me.

rhyme scheme *ABCDEC FGHIH JKLLK*

Line 4 of the middle stanza uses a device called internal rhyme. (Did you notice "exes" rhymes with "Texas"?)

EATING MY WORDS • BRIAN P. CLEARY

TO E. E. CUMMINGS

thank you for your lively verse
and playful, quirky prose.
you wrote of nature, war, and love,
the

r
a
i
n
d
r
o
p
s

and the rose.

a modern-thinking artist,
with an intellect immense,
if you're not in every classroom,
it's a capital offense.

thank you for undreary theory,
style, wit, and grace.
your books are always on my shelf
(tucked in my lower case).

rhyme scheme *ABCB DEFE* . . .

E. E. Cummings was a poet and modern artist who used punctuation and type in interesting and nontraditional ways. He would often put "non" or "un" in front of a word, as in the final stanza of this poem. Do you get the double meaning of "lower case" in the last line?

Line 1 of the last stanza uses a device called internal rhyme. (Did you notice "undreary" rhymes with "theory"?)

SLEEPOVER PARTY

The letters had a sleepover
with popcorn, snacks, and TV.
But drinking too much soda
Made the elemeno P.

rhyme scheme *ABCB*

A quatrain is a four-line verse that usually rhymes. It could be just one stanza (like a paragraph of poetry) in a longer poem or the entire poem. Quatrains come in more than ten possible rhyme schemes or patterns.

I BABYSAT (ONCE)

I was pushing the buggy one day,
when my grip on the handle gave way,
and it started to roll
downhill out of control,
with my sister still snoozing away.

She rolled through the center of town,
still asleep through the deafening sound,
of barks and bowwows
of the beagles, Chihuahuas,
and mutts at the city dog pound.

Past Main Street and Elm rolled my sister.
It's amazing that all the cars missed her.
She moved with the ease
of a cool evening breeze
but the speed of a level 3 twister.

I found her off Highway 19,
having gone through a car wash machine.
With a lemony smell
(they had waxed her as well),
I brought her back home nice and clean.

rhyme scheme *AABBA CCDDC* . . .

Limericks are often funny five-line poems that were popularized
by English artist and poet Edward Lear. Lines 1, 2, and 5 rhyme
with one another, and lines 3 and 4 are shorter and rhyme with
each other, but not the other three lines.

AT SUMMER CAMP

Beestings and mosquito bites,
centipedes and lice and mites,
heat and sunburn, ancient rafts,
making lots of useless crafts,
slugs and bugs and spiders creeping
homesick bunkmate's nightly weeping,
waking up to shrieking whistles,
getting pricked among the thistles,
heavy backpacks, soggy shoes,
tiny cuts that itch and ooze,
corny songs and no TVs,
hives of hornets, wasps, and bees.
Camp can surely be a bummer;
can't wait till I come back next summer!

rhyme scheme *AABBCCDD* . . .

EATING MY WORDS • BRIAN P. CLEARY

WHERE I'M FROM

I am from baseball cards and bubble gum.
I am from the smells of coffee cake,
bacon, and freshly painted walls.
I am from Friday night football
and Sunday morning mass.
I am from strong women
and men who can't make a long story short.
I am from, "If you don't go to school, you can't go to basketball."
I am from black-and-white TV, Beatles records,
and tuna noodle casserole.

A "Where I'm From" poem is a style of list poem. If you look up this form online, you'll find prompts for specific lines to include, such as "list two family traits," "describe your home to someone who has never seen it," or "what are some rules you have in your house?"

List poems, as the name suggests, are made up of lists of things, places, people, colors, emotions, sounds, events, and more. Some rhyme and some don't, and they can make you think, smile, squirm, giggle, nod your head, or sigh.

IT COULD BE WORSE

Cleaning the litter box, scooping and sifting,
I gag as I whisper a vow:
I'll never ask my mother or dad
if I can adopt a pet cow.

rhyme scheme *ABCB*

QUADRUPLICATES

Frankie was born at ten twenty-seven,
and Xochitl at ten thirty-four.
Teddy was born at half past eleven,
and Elaina arrived just before.

rhyme scheme *ABAB*

A quatrain is a four-line verse that usually rhymes. It could be just
one stanza (like a paragraph of poetry) in a longer poem or the
entire poem. Quatrains come in more than ten possible rhyme
schemes or patterns.

HOME

I went to school in Paris. I went to school in Turkey.
A half a year in London, Omaha, and Albuquerque.
I went to school in China, New Delhi, and in Guam,
and for a little while, I went to school in Vietnam.

I went to school in Sicily; then after that, Sri Lanka.
I spent a very chilly wintertime in Minnetonka.
I went to school in Amsterdam, in Hamburg, and in Rome.
As long as I had books with me, I always felt at home.

rhyme scheme *AABB CCDD*

Feminine rhyme is a rhyme of two or more syllables in which the first syllable is the strongest, such as Turkey and Albuquerque.

MY BROTHER JOE

My brother Joe steals.
My brother Joe hits.
I know he's not safe when he's out.
There's sometimes foul play
in the things that he does.
Can you tell what I'm talking about?

rhyme scheme *ABCDEC*

This poem is also a riddle. For you to solve it, you need to know two meanings for some of the words.

MAKING RIPPLES

 out and look up **2** the morning **SK+** 👁

 each day, &

ask yourself what **U** 🥫 do @ school, @ 🏠 , @ play

2 make this day a better **1**

 some **1** **N+** 👂 or far,

a better **PL+** ♠ because of who **U R** .

This type of picture poem is called a rebus. A rebus can take the form of a poem (as it does here), a paragraph, a sentence, or even a riddle. Some of the words or syllables are replaced by pictures or symbols. Can you translate it?

JOY

Joy looks like fireworks against a night sky.
Joy tastes like the first crunch into an ear of corn.
Joy sounds like a crowd on a roller coaster.
Joy smells like popcorn.
Joy feels like running home on the last day of school.

A sensory poem uses the five senses. The poem starts with an abstract subject (something you can't feel or see, such as anger, fear, happiness, or peace) and tells the reader how the subject looks, tastes, smells, feels, and sounds. The title is also the first word of each sentence.

STORY PROBLEM

If a train leaves the ocean at 10 seconds per ounce, and
    the train makes 27 stops daily,
Then how many yards of spaghetti sauce is needed . . .
    to spray paint your great-grandpa's ukulele?

rhyme scheme *AA*

A doha is a form often used by Hindi poets. It is written in couplets with twenty-four syllables in each line (thirteen syllables before a pause, and eleven after).

TRANSLATION

When Teddy says he "shook a tower,"
what he means is "took a shower."

He'll point and say, "a flutter by,"
and then we'll see a butterfly.

But when he says he "pepped in stew,"
we'll tell him he should wipe his shoe.

rhyme scheme *AA BB CC*

A spoonerism mixes up the initial
sounds of two or more words. It gets its
name from William Archibald Spooner,
a minister and educator who was famous
for this type of verbal slipup.

A couplet consists of two lines of verse that typically
have the same meter and rhyme at the end.

IN THE POCKETS OF MY CARGO SHORTS

A photo of my schnauzer, Dave, and one of Richard Nixon,
a cell phone from eight years ago that needs a little fixin',
half a double cheeseburger, half a pint of soup,
a soggy, old toupee I found that smells a bit like poop.
A deck of cards, eleven cents, a salamander, dice,
seashells, a harmonica that's old but pretty nice.
Duct tape, Scotch tape, French tape, and a yo-yo (minus string).
What's inside my pockets? Well, you might say everything.

rhyme scheme *AABBCCDD*

> A couplet consists of two lines of verse that typically have the same meter and rhyme at the end.

EATING MY WORDS • BRIAN P. CLEARY

LOVE AND PEACE

Tyler likes Hannah.
Hannah like Lance.
Lance likes the kid
with the leopard print pants.
They like Isaiah.
Isaiah likes Tess.
She likes Antonio,
Justin, and Jess.
Chris likes Melissa,
who just likes to dance.
Shelly likes David,
and David likes Vance.
There's love in the air
of Room 229,
but peace is a little bit
harder to find.

rhyme scheme *ABCBDEFE* . . .

Trochaic refers to a poetic meter pattern that begins with a stressed, or emphasized, syllable followed by an unstressed, or softer, syllable. Example: Brian (BRI-an) has one stressed syllable, followed by one that is unstressed.

List poems, as the name suggests, are made up of lists of things, places, people, colors, emotions, sounds, events, and more. Some rhyme and some don't, and they can make you think, smile, squirm, giggle, nod your head, or sigh.

YOU'RE SUPPOSED TO BE YOU

You're supposed to be you—
it's kind of your job.
You're not to be Lou
or Mackenzie or Bob.

You're not to be Mary
or Michael or Sue.
You're not to be Harry
or Lizzy but you.

If you're somebody else,
then there will be two
of that somebody else—
but zero of you.

rhyme scheme *ABAB CACA DADA*

A quatrain is a four-line verse that usually rhymes. It could be just one stanza (like a paragraph of poetry) in a longer poem or the entire poem. Quatrains come in more than ten possible rhyme schemes or patterns.

EATING MY WORDS • BRIAN P. CLEARY

AT THE SHORE

Deep in the summertime, late in the day,
the salt water laps at the pier by the bay.
A sliver above throws a wink of moonlight.
The wind in the willow trees whispers good night.

rhyme scheme *AABB*

I WISH I HAD MY BIRTHDAY TEN TIMES YEARLY

I wish I had my birthday ten times yearly
with ice cream, cake, and presents by the mountain.
And people singing to me quite sincerely,
some party games, perhaps a soda fountain.
I'd have my favorite dinner ten times yearly.
But when I pause to do a little countin',
and I multiply the numbers up—oh, wow—
I'd be something like one hundred ten by now!

rhyme scheme *ABABABCC*

A rispetto is an Italian poetic form. It is typically composed of eight hendecasyllabic (eleven-syllable) lines. Early rispetto poems typically had a rhyme scheme of *ABABABCC*.

THE DAY THE COMMAS CALLED IN SICK

I love eating
my favorite books
my cat
and my Auntie Ellen.

Free verse is a form of poetry that does not rhyme or have a regular meter to it.

Enjambment is the continuation of a sentence from one line or stanza of a poem to the next. The words "run over" or "spill over" from one line to the next. Lines without enjambment are called end-stopped.

FORTY

Forty—
spelled so strangely.
Ten times the number four,
yet, where's the *u*? What did they do
to U?

The American cinquain is an unrhymed poetic form with five lines, each of which has specific syllable counts. Line 1 has two syllables, line 2 has four, line 3 has six, line 4 has eight, and line 5 has two. And why do we spell forty without the *u*? Maybe U can find out.

HOW TO WRITE A COW POEM

Writing cow poems is so simple:
just "milk" the puns for all they're worth,
and try to make it "moo-ving."
Mention "over the moon"
in one of the lines,
say "udderly,"
then end with,
"that's no
bull!"

A nonet is a nine-line poem with specific descending syllable counts for each line. Line 1 has nine syllables, line 2 has eight, line 3 has seven, etc. The final line is only one syllable.

GRANDPA'S HANDS

Grandpa's hands
fix screen doors
and plant mums . . .

make cookies,
clap for me,
and deal cards.

Grandpa's hands
pray, throw darts,
and hold mine.

A tricube is a poem with three stanzas,
each consisting of three lines. Each line
has three syllables.

OUR ALPHABETICAL CLASSROOM

Alison's a chatterbox. Ben is always crying.
Chloe smells like chicken soup, and Dylan's often lying.
Ethan holds his breath sometimes until he's red and florid.
Fiona drew another set of eyebrows on her for'ead.

Gracie is the teacher's pet. Henry clicks his braces.
Izzy's chair is always damp whenever we switch places.
Jude is late most every day, and Kylie loves the drama.
Logan can't be more than twenty paces from his mama.

Maddie spills most everything, and Nicholas is pushy.
Oscar taped a "kick me" sign on his own little tushy.
Pat and Quinn both interrupt, and Riley likes to tell.
Sophie's always bossing us, and Taylor is as well.

EATING MY WORDS • BRIAN P. CLEARY

Ursula cannot recall a thing that she's been taught.
Vicki hums a little tune whenever deep in thought.
Wyatt's always bragging that he has eleven toes
and makes a little whistling sound when breathing out his nose.

Xavier taps the gerbil cage and just ignores the teacher.
Yosef does it too and even climbed in with the creature.
Zadie has a made-up friend to chat with, text, and call.
And though our class sounds sort of strange, I kind of like them all!

rhyme scheme *AABB CCDD* . . .

List poems, as the name suggests, are made up of lists of things, places, people, colors, emotions, sounds, events, and more. Some rhyme and some don't, and they can make you think, smile, squirm, giggle, nod your head, or sigh.

MY CAT BYTES

Some cats like to prowl, and some even growl,
while others would rather take naps.
But my Mrs. Mittens—an internet kitten—is
fonder of laptops than laps.

Unlike other cats, this one downloads and chats
and is constantly checking her email.
An ad she has posted has recently boasted
she's a young, single, Siamese female.

With paws soft and quick, she'll type and she'll click,
do some research or maybe some shopping.
She bookmarks new sites. She surfs and she writes,
or she'll scan in some photos for swapping.

It's simply absurd. She's an internet nerd,
who ignores all the rest of the house.
What cat would admit it would ever see fit
to enjoy so much time with a mouse?

rhyme scheme *ABCB DEFE . . .*

> This poem uses a device called internal rhyme. (Did you notice "prowl" rhymes with "growl" in line 1?)

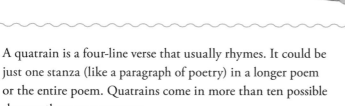

> A quatrain is a four-line verse that usually rhymes. It could be just one stanza (like a paragraph of poetry) in a longer poem or the entire poem. Quatrains come in more than ten possible rhyme schemes or patterns.

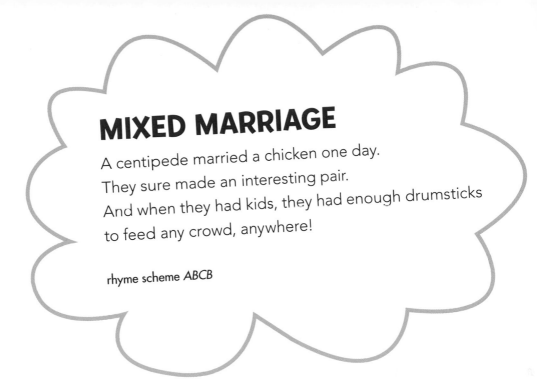

MIXED MARRIAGE

A centipede married a chicken one day.
They sure made an interesting pair.
And when they had kids, they had enough drumsticks
to feed any crowd, anywhere!

rhyme scheme *ABCB*

NOSE FLOOD

"I chuckled so hard, milk came out of my nose,"
said my math teacher, Mrs. Mantunkenny.
"What's hard to explain," she said with some pain,
"is that I had not even drunk any."

rhyme scheme *ABCB*

Iambic refers to a poetic meter pattern that begins with an unstressed syllable followed by a stressed, or stronger, syllable. Example: the word *vanilla* (va-NIL-la). That's an unstressed syllable followed by a stressed, or stronger, one.

Line 3 uses a device called internal rhyme. (Did you notice "explain" rhymes with "pain"?)

MY BEAGLE'S BREATH SMELLS NOTHING LIKE A ROSE

My beagle's breath smells nothing like a rose.
Her "sit," and "fetch" and "down" look much the same.
On floors she leaves a wetness for my toes,
and rarely will she answer to her name.

She couldn't aid someone who cannot see
or help police or fire teams patrol.
If tasked with herding sheep, she'd likely flee
to run about or nap or dig a hole.

A robin's chirp is sweeter than her bark:
a yodel or a howl, low and deep.
She's not the best-behaved dog at the park.
At night she wants to play when she should sleep.

Yet each day I return from school, it's she
who's happy and excited to see me.

rhyme scheme *ABAB CDCD EFEF GG*

A Shakespearean sonnet, or English sonnet, was often used by William Shakespeare. It's made up of three quatrains plus a couplet at the end. It is written in a meter called iambic pentameter. Each ten-syllable line contains five pairs of unstressed/stressed syllables called iambs.

IF I COULD DUNK A BASKETBALL

If I could dunk a basketball,
I'd want to play every waking minute.
You'd find me dunking on courts, playgrounds, and driveways,
like I was dipping a cookie into a glass of milk.

I'd want to play every waking minute,
soaring toward the hoop with ease,
like I was dipping a cookie into a glass of milk,
I'd be cooler than the other side of my pillow.

Soaring toward the hoop with ease,
that's how I'd spend my days and nights.
I'd be cooler than the other side of my pillow
if I could dunk a basketball.

> The pantoum originated in Malaysia. Some pantoums rhyme and
> others, like this one, don't, but here are the basic rules: each stanza has
> four lines, and the second and fourth lines of every stanza are used as
> the first and third lines of the next stanza. The last line of a pantoum is
> frequently identical to the first.

I'VE GOT YOUR NUMBER

Sweeter than some pie I (2 × 4),
You're funny, smart, and kind.
You're heavenly (9 - 7) look at,
And you're off (20 ÷ 2) on my mind.

More talented than Erin, Kaylee,
Madison, and Kath.
Are you the perfect (6 - 5) (2 × 2) me?
Honey, do the math.

rhyme scheme *ABCB DEDE*

By solving these simple math problems, you'll find the missing words to the verse. Although the numbers aren't spelled identically to the missing words, you should be able to get the meaning. At least one of the solutions is a homophone.

DEAD TO ME

As I wear my new
sneakers out of the shoe store,
my old ones, muddy,
torn, and worn are placed in the
shoebox—a cardboard coffin.

EATING MY WORDS • BRIAN P. CLEARY

IT'S PRETTY SIMPLE

Is it *its* . . . or is it *it's*?
They're oftentimes confused.
But when it's a contraction—
an apostrophe is used.
It's always just a shorter form
of "it is" or "it has,"
like "It's a girl!" or "Gosh, it's been
so rainy out"; whereas,
its is a possessive word:
"Its surface is so sticky."
Grammar and its many rules
can be a little tricky.

rhyme scheme *ABCBDEFE* . . .

This brief poem also includes a number of other literary devices, including personification, alliteration, enjambment, and metaphor—a direct comparison of two things without the use of "like" or "as."

A tanka is a traditional Japanese form of poetry consisting of thirty-one syllables written in a single, unbroken line. In English translations, the tanka tends to take on a five-line form with the following syllable counts: five/seven/five/seven/seven.

IN A FIX

I was never much for school,
I'm Penelope O'Toole,
custodian at PS 104.
I'd rather stand than sit,
and I like to talk a bit,
while pacing back and forth across the floor.

While it's true, I'd squirm and fuss
from the time I'd leave the bus,
I guess I just liked "doing" with my hands.
And I think it's rather cool
that now I'm "back in school"
and in charge of all its maintenance demands.

Like these:
I'm very adept with
a quarter-inch ratchet.
I'm good with a chain saw,
a hammer, and hatchet.

I can fix a compressor,
a lock, or a door hinge,
I can take something purple
and paint it bright orange.

The meter or "beat" of
this poem shifts from one
rhyming and rhythmic
pattern to another one.
Can you see at which
point it switches?

If something needs winding
or grinding or mixing,
if it's due for a polish, a shine,
or just fixing,

if it needs to be soldered
or watered or oiled,
if it's busted or rusted or
rotten or soiled,

they don't call someone
with a Yale PhD—
they call and they text
and they shout out for me!

rhyme scheme for stanzas 1–2 *AABCCB DDEAAE*

rhyme scheme for stanzas 3–8 *ABCB DEFE* . . .

The second portion of this poem is a list poem. List poems, as the name
suggests, are made up of lists of things, places, people, colors, emotions,
sounds, events, and more. Some rhyme and some don't, and they can make
you think, smile, squirm, giggle, nod your head, or sigh.

MY FATHER'S MUSTACHE

My father's mustache is the largest in town.
It's bigger than all of the others.
It grows all along the width of his face
and continues right on to his brother's.

rhyme scheme *ABCB*

FIVE

Max has got three extra legs
(one right and two above).
He has some trouble walking,
but his pants fit like a glove.

rhyme scheme *ABCB*

Similes compare two unlike things (such as your mom and an ox) using the words "like" or "as." "My mom is strong as an ox," is an example of a simile.

MAKE A WISH

My pet dragon's birthday is today, and she's excited.
She'll make a wish and blow, and all the candles will be lighted.

rhyme scheme *AA*

A couplet consists of two lines of verse that typically have the same meter and rhyme at the end.

MS. GARCIA AND ONOMATOPOEIA

My teacher, Ms. Garcia,
loves onomatopoeia.
Each clippity-clop
and each cackle.
Each ding and each drip.
Every flop and
each flip.
Each clank, every click,
and each crackle.

She adores all the hiccups,
each howl and hush.
It jingles her jangles for real.
Every squawk, every squeak,
and each clunk, crack, and creak,
she smiles and lets out a squeal.

rhyme scheme for stanza 1 *AABCCB*

rhyme scheme for stanza 2 *DEFGGF*

Onomatopoeia is a word that mimics the sound of the thing
it refers to. Examples: howl, swish, clunk.

I SPOTTED A LEOPARD

I spotted a leopard
(or so I believed).
I spotted a leopard one day.
I thought I'd be famous
for what I achieved,
but it turns out they're *all* born that way.

rhyme scheme *ABCDBC*

This poem employs the use of wordplay. Do you get the two meanings of "spotted"?

SNOW DAY

Precipitation
can mean vacation.

rhyme scheme *AA*

SCENES FROM THE HALLWAY

Madison, Mason, and Mia are laughing.
Harper is hanging with Hannah.
Mr. Foxx fixes the flickering light
by the classroom of Mrs. Santana.

Riley and Remi are flirting a bit.
Fiona can't find her new phone.
Jackson and Jenni and Jaden are running,
and Scarlett is scarfing a scone.

The hallways are hopping, it's lively and loud,
but it's soon to be silent as snow.
The lockers will latch, and the students will sigh,
and then off to their classes they'll go.

rhyme scheme *ABCB DEFE* . . .

Alliteration refers to repetition of the same sound (often the same letter) in the beginning of words that are near one another. Did you notice how words beginning with *M, H, F, R, F, J, Sc, S, L,* and *Th* are used in this poem? This use of alliteration is a form of wordplay.

Did you also spot the simile? Similes compare two unlike things (such as your mom and an ox) using the words "like" or "as." "My mom is strong as an ox" is an example of a simile.

MY DREAM IN RHYME

An Asian
dragon
in a
station
wagon
gave
a limp
pansy
to a
chim-
panzee.

rhyme scheme AABB

Enjambment is the continuation of a sentence from one line or stanza of a poem to the next. The words "run over" or "spill over" from one line to the next. Lines without enjambment are called end-stopped.

IT'S COMPLICATED

Born in Minneapolis, my loving father was.
He stayed there till the age of seventeen.
Mother started life out as a young Chicago lass,
a more midwestern girl you'd never seen.

They met in West Milwaukee while they were both in school,
got married, then settled there with me.
Things were calm and peaceful, to begin with (so I hear),
in this tiny little family of three.

My folks agree on child-rearing practices and such,
on politics, nutrition, and religion.
But there's a certain topic on which they disagree
and neither one of them will move a smidgen.

On football season Sundays, my mom wears navy blue;
she'll watch Chicago's game downstairs and scream.
With painted-purple face, my dad puts on his game upstairs.
He's cheering for his Minnesota team.

Republican and Democrat? Protestant and Jew?
The differences in couples can be striking.
But those are hardly noticed when compared to what I've got,
where Mother is a Bear and Dad's a Viking.

rhyme scheme *ABCB DEFE* . . .

This is an example of wordplay, and the words chosen are specifically to pick up on the double meaning of bear and Viking, the animal and seafaring historical figure, and Bear and Viking, the players and fans of professional football teams from Chicago and Minnesota, respectively.

CAN'T WAIT TILL NEXT YEAR

(Sung to the tune of the song "Oh! Susanna")

Oh, I went to see Great-Grandma
with my whole big family.
Uncle George and my Aunt Anna
even brought their chimpanzee.

My Auntie Peg
will juggle cleavers—
three or four or five,
and my cousin Jake,
he'll take a rake
and poke a big beehive.

Thanks, Great-Grandma,
you're lovely, kind, and dear,
and I'm sure we'll come next summer if
we just survive this year!

rhyme scheme *ABCB DEFE* . . .

I wrote this little poem to the tune of a popular folk song from the 1800s. Can you sing the tune and read the words?

Lines 1 and 3 in the first stanza use a device called near rhyme, which you'll often find in songs. (Did you catch that "Great-Grandma" and "Aunt Anna" sound similar?)

Lines 4 and 5 in the second stanza use a device called internal rhyme. (Did you notice "Jake" rhymes with "rake"?)

CAT-ATONIC

When Mr. Foaley slowly
moved his roly-poly cat,
he found eight kittens, small as mittens,
beneath her roll of fat!
Four shy, four bold,
the tiny fold would roll and squirm and play
while mother ate and tried to sleep,
for she'd had quite a day.

rhyme scheme *ABCBDEFE*

In this brief poem, there are (believe it or not) examples of each of the following: noun, verb, adjective, article, pronoun, preposition, adverb, simile, synonym, antonym, conjunction, homonym, homophone, rhyme, and alliteration. How many can you find?

Lines 1, 2, and 3 use a device called internal rhyme. (Did you notice "Foaley" rhymes with "slowly" and "roly-poly"?)

A RECIPE FOR POETRY

A quarter cup of rhyming pairs—
One pinch alliteration,
a dash of macaronic verse,
complete with full translation,
a tablespoon of parody,
a teaspoon of acrostic,
a pinch of jokes or wordplay
to ensure it's not too caustic.
A haiku or a concrete poem,
a sonnet, long and rosy,
a simile or metaphor
that's funny, sweet, or prose-y.
Half an ounce of limerick,
a lantern and a riddle.
Layer them across the top,
the bottom, and the middle.
Shake it, then you bake it,
then you slice it up in thirds,
frost it up with icing next—
it's time to eat your words!

rhyme scheme *ABCBDEFE* . . .

GLOSSARY OF POETIC TERMS

acrostic: a poem in which a particular set of letters—most often the first letter of each line—spells out a word or phrase. The word or phrase it spells out is called the *acrostich*, and it is usually the subject of the piece.

alliteration: repetition of the same sound (often the same letter) in the beginning of words that are near one another

American cinquain: an unrhymed poetic form with five lines, each of which have specific syllable counts. Line 1 has two syllables, line 2 has four, line 3 has six, line 4 has eight, and line 5 has two.

blues: an African American musical art form. The first and second lines in each verse are typically identical, and the subject of the song usually has to do with something that makes the singer sad or "blue."

concrete poem: a poem with a shape that resembles the subject of the poem. The letters, words, or symbols are arranged on the page to make a picture.

couplet: two lines of verse that typically have the same meter and rhyme at the end

doha: a form often used by Hindi poets. It is written in couplets with twenty-four syllables in each line (thirteen syllables before a pause and eleven after)

enjambment: the continuation of a sentence from one line or stanza of a poem to the next. The words "run over" or "spill over" from one line to the next. Lines without enjambment are called end-stopped.

feminine rhyme: a rhyme of two or more syllables in which the first syllable is the strongest

free verse: a form of poetry that does not rhyme or have a regular meter to it

haiku: a three-line poetic form that originated in Japan. Line 1 has five syllables, line 2 has seven, and the final line has five. Think of a haiku as a sandwich, with the five-syllable lines as the bread and the seven-syllable line as the stuff in the middle. Traditionally, haiku have nature as their subject.

iambic: a poetic meter pattern that begins with an unstressed syllable followed by a stressed, or stronger, syllable. Example: the word *vanilla* (va-NIL-la). That's an unstressed syllable followed by a stressed, or stronger, one.

internal rhyme: two or more rhyming words in the same line

jump rope rhyme: also called a skipping rope rhyme. The rhythm of the jump rope's rotation is synced to the rhythm or the beat of the rhymed verse.

lantern: sometimes spelled lanturne or lanterne, this poem is a short, Japanese form of poetry. Line 1 consists of a one-syllable noun (person, place, or thing). That noun is the subject of the poem. The following lines describe that subject—or as the name *lantern* suggests, "shed light" on it. Line 2 has two syllables. Line 3 has three syllables. Line 4 has four. Line 5 goes back to one syllable. All lines are centered on the page, so the finished poem roughly resembles the shape of a Japanese lantern.

limerick: an often funny five-line poem with a rhyme scheme of *AABBA* that was popularized by English artist and poet Edward Lear. Lines 1, 2, and 5 rhyme with one another, and lines 3 and 4 are shorter and rhyme with each other, but not the other three lines.

list poem: poems made up of lists of things, places, people, colors, emotions, sounds, events, and more. Some rhyme and some don't, and they can make you think, smile, squirm, giggle, nod your head, or sigh.

macaronic verse: a rhyming poem that includes words from other languages

masculine rhyme: occurs when the rhyming words either have one syllable (example: "Ruth" and "truth"), or when the rhyme is in the final syllable of a multisyllable word or phrase ("direct" and "respect" or "to sleep" and "to sweep")

meter: the rhythm or beat of a poem, which is created by the pattern of stressed and unstressed syllables a poet uses

naani: an Indian poetic form that has four lines, a total of between twenty and twenty-five syllables, and is often about relationships

near rhyme: rhyming in which the words sound similar but are not an exact rhyme

nonet: a nine-line poem with specific descending syllable counts for each line. Line 1 has nine syllables, line 2 has eight, line 3 has seven, etc. The final line is only one syllable.

onomatopoeia: a word that mimics the sound of the thing it refers to. Examples: howl, swish, clunk.

palindrome: a word or phrase that is spelled the same way backward and forward. A palindrome can be a phrase like "a Toyota," a word like "kayak," a name like "Hannah," or even a number like "747."

pantoum: a poetic form that originated in Malaysia. Each stanza has four lines, and the second and fourth lines of every stanza are used as the first and third lines of the next stanza. The last line of a pantoum is frequently identical to the first. Some pantoums rhyme and others don't.

personification: giving human qualities to a nonliving object, such as a bus or a guitar. Examples: "The sky cried," or "The bus wheezed to a stop."

pun: a verbal joke or play on words that uses words or phrases with multiple meanings, often with a humorous result

quatrain: a four-line verse that usually rhymes. It could be just one stanza (like a paragraph of poetry) in a longer poem or the entire poem. Quatrains come in more than ten possible rhyme schemes or patterns.

rebus: a type of picture poem. It can take the form of a poem, a paragraph, a sentence, or even a riddle. Some of the words or syllables are replaced by pictures or symbols.

rispetto: an Italian poetic form. It is typically composed of eight hendecasyllabic (eleven-syllable) lines. Early rispetto poems typically had a rhyme scheme of *ABABABCC*.

sensory poem: a poem that uses the five senses. It starts with an abstract subject (something you can't feel or see, such as happiness or peace) and tells the reader how the subject looks, tastes, smells, feels, and sounds. The title is also the first word of each sentence.

Shakespearean sonnet: also called an English sonnet. It was often used by William Shakespeare. It's made up of three quatrains plus a couplet at the end. The rhyme scheme for this type of poem is *ABAB CDCD EFEF GG*. It is written in a meter called iambic pentameter. Each ten-syllable line contains five pairs of unstressed/stressed syllables called iambs.

simile: comparing two unlike things using the words "like" or "as"

spoonerism: mixing up the initial sounds of two or more words. It gets its name from William Archibald Spooner, a minister and educator who was famous for this type of verbal slipup.

syllable: a part of a word that has a single vowel sound and is pronounced in one beat. For example, "play" has one syllable and "playground" has two.

tanka: a traditional Japanese poetic form consisting of thirty-one syllables written in a single, unbroken line. In English translations, the tanka tends to take on a five-line form with the following syllable counts: five/seven/five/seven/seven.

tricube: a poem with three stanzas, each consisting of three lines. Each line has three syllables.

trochaic: a poetic meter pattern that begins with a stressed, or emphasized, syllable, followed by an unstressed, or softer, syllable. Example: Brian (BRI-an) has one stressed syllable followed by one that is unstressed.

villanelle: a French form of poetry that is nineteen lines long. Line 1 is repeated on lines 6, 12, and 18. Line 3 is repeated on lines 9, 15, and 19. The second line of each stanza rhymes all the way through the poem.

Where I'm From: a style of list poem that describes a person's background, heritage, or history

wordplay: a humorous device that might employ puns, rhyme, alliteration, or other literary tools for comic effect

FURTHER READING

Fletcher, Ralph J. *Poetry Matters: Writing a Poem from the Inside Out*. New York: HarperTrophy, 2002.

Harris, Chris. *My Head Has a Bellyache: More Nonsense for Mischievous Kids and Immature Grown-Ups*. New York: Little, Brown, 2023.

Herrera, Juan Felipe. *Jabberwalking*. Somerville, MA: Candlewick, 2018.

Latham, Irene, and Charles Waters. *Dictionary for a Better World: Poems, Quotes, and Anecdotes from A to Z*. Minneapolis: Carolrhoda Books, 2020.

Livingston, Myra Cohn. *Poem-Making: Ways to Begin Writing Poetry*. New York: HarperCollins, 1991.

Nesbitt, Kenn, ed. *One Minute Till Bedtime: 60-Second Poems to Send You Off to Sleep*. New York: Little, Brown, 2016.

Prelutsky, Jack. *A Pizza the Size of the Sun*. New York: Greenwillow, 1996.

Random House. *Random House Webster's Rhyming Dictionary*. New York: Random House Reference, 2008.

Silverstein, Shel. *Where the Sidewalk Ends*. New York: HarperCollins, 1974.

INDEX OF POETIC FORMS

acrostic, 15, 32, 50, 66, 115
alliteration, 10, 31, 58, 64, 103, 110, 114, 115
American cinquain, 93

blues, 52

concrete, 19, 37, 115
couplet, 40, 53, 87–88, 97, 100, 107

doha, 86

enjambment, 17, 93, 103, 111

feminine rhyme, 24, 71, 83
free verse, 41, 93

haiku, 21, 38, 57, 115

iambic, 46, 99, 100
internal rhyme, 59, 68, 71, 76–77, 98–99, 113–114

jump rope rhyme, 35

lantern, 20, 115
limerick, 9, 26, 45, 60, 61, 71, 79, 115
list poem, 10, 29, 47, 49, 63, 73, 81, 89, 97, 105

macaronic verse, 25, 115
masculine rhyme, 48
meter, 24, 40–41, 46, 53, 69, 74, 87–89, 93, 97, 99–100, 104

naani, 17
near rhyme, 113
nonet, 94

onomatopoeia, 108

palindrome, 13
pantoum, 101
personification, 33, 103
pun, 22–23, 34, 40–41, 58, 64, 67, 75, 94

quatrain, 12, 31, 48–49, 64, 74, 78, 82, 90, 98, 100

rebus, 85
rispetto, 92

sensory poem, 86
Shakespearean sonnet, 100
simile, 16, 106, 110, 114–115
spoonerism, 87

tanka, 103
tricube, 95
trochaic, 24, 69, 74, 89

villanelle, 34

Where I'm From, 81
wordplay, 7, 58, 64, 109–110, 112, 115